Discovery and Adventure

Written by:
Bill Radley

Editor:
Valerie Peters

General Editor:
Ron Jeffries

Illustration:
Peter Harrison
Bill Radley

Photographs:
Bren Neal

Design:
Colin Watson

The Scout Association,
Baden-Powell House,
Queen's Gate, London SW7 5JS

SBN 85165 077 5

First Edition
First Printing
August 1973

Second Printing
October 1974

Printed in Great Britain by
Kent Paper Company Ltd, London and Ashford, Kent

Contents

Foreword

GOD says: I like youngsters. I want people to be like them.
I don't like old people unless they are still children.
I want only children in my kingdom; this has been decreed from the beginning of time.
Youngsters—twisted, humped, wrinkled, white-bearded—all kinds of youngsters, but youngsters.
There is no changing it, it has been decided, there is room for no one else. . . .
. . . I like youngsters because they are still struggling, because they are still sinning.
Not because they sin—if you understand me—but because they know that they sin, and they say so, and they try not to sin any more. . . .
. . . But above all, I like youngsters because of the look in their eyes. In their eyes I can read their age.
In my heaven, there will be only five-year-old eyes, for I know of nothing more beautiful than the pure eyes of a child.
It is not surprising, for I live in children, and it is I who look out through their eyes. . . .
. . . Hurry! Now is the time. I am ready to give you again the beautiful face of a child, the beautiful eyes of a child. . . .
For I love youngsters, and I want everyone to be like them.

Extracts from *Prayers of Life*
Michel Quoist

Cub Scouts join our movement for enjoyment and so we must make our programmes as full of fun as possible. Discovery and adventure should be the themes when we plan the Pack meeting. This book contains some programmes to use at ordinary Pack meetings or at special evening or weekend meetings. The first chapter **'Voyage of Discovery'** is an example of a weekend programme which has already been proved a success; the other chapters all contain projects which have been successfully used, but these have been split into categories and the leader can sort out his own programme from these—adapting it to his own ideas. At the end of the book there are some guidelines to programme planning which may help you to decide how to go about using the various projects and, indeed, how to think of your own.

All the material is especially intended for Cub Scouts with handicaps, since they can derive great benefit from Scouting projects which they find enjoyable.

Although ample supervision and help are necessary, the youngsters must be allowed to carry out as much of the work as possible.

A background of music can be helpful as this helps to stimulate the boy, and slow learners are able to respond especially well to this. Give the youngsters every opportunity to make exciting models and collages and I am certain that you will be amazed by the results. An example of what can be achieved will be seen by the children's drawings of 'People Around the World' in the first chapter.

In the games sessions shown, some games must obviously be adapted to cater for the individual disability of the boy, but nevertheless Cubs with handicaps still enjoy competitive games.

In ball games, for example, use a beach ball or a balloon (having first made certain that none of the children will be frightened by bursting balloons). Games such as Kim's Game, identification of sounds, dice games and any other games where time is not a factor are excellent.*

The stories which start each chapter are meant to be used as the central point or focus of the programme. They should furnish you and the youngsters with the ideas to set your imagination going. They are not intended to be read out word for word at the beginning of the programme, but should be told or used in any way that you require. Many of the projects have been combined boy and girl schemes and if you have a Pack Holiday Centre with accommodation which can be divided, this is a very good idea. Failing this, an afternoon project with boys and girls could prove rewarding. Do try, but remember that the end result must be **'fun'**, and bring a little laughter and happiness into the lives of these youngsters.

*See the book *Cub Scout Games* published by **The Scout Association,** for further ideas.

A Treasure Chest

IN planning programmes with Cubs you should try to use as many new ideas and new materials as possible.

In all Training:

If we only listen—we tend to forget.
If we can see—we understand.
But if we do—we know and remember.

Therefore if visual aids are used training can be incorporated in a variety of activities which to the Cubs will all be part of the fun.

When we think of programmes involving handcrafts a number of factors tend to put us off, namely:

1. **Lack of space.**
2. **That we might make a mess.**
3. **The cost of materials.**
4. **Knowing where to start.**

These are but minor problems. Storage space necessary for the finished items can be worked out before they are made.

Covering the floor and tables with old newspapers will reduce the amount of mess and all scraps can then be rolled up and thrown away.

Materials do not need to cost very much. Start collecting bits and pieces—eggboxes, matchboxes, washing-up liquid bottles, old pieces of wallpaper, material etc.

Start in a small way, but plan what you are going to do and prepare your materials accordingly. It is preferable that each Cub should finish the handcraft item in an evening, and not continue it over a number of weeks.

Some boys will naturally produce good results, but the majority will produce good or bad results depending upon the way in which they react to their work. Your enthusiasm will do much to encourage them to better efforts.

You should try to see possibilities everywhere, try new methods, new forms, new materials and, indeed, build up a treasure chest of ideas and materials.

A box of equipment is a good idea and this can be added to all the time. Here is a check list of some general items you may want:

Scissors—at least a dozen pairs
Staples
Stapler
Rulers
Compasses
Good supply of glue
Poster paints
Brushes
Crayons
Felt tipped pens
Pencils
A good supply of cartridge paper
Cardboard sheets
Doodling pad
Plenty of string
Odd pieces of rope
Wrapping paper

and here is a list of some items you could collect:
eggboxes; matchboxes; cardboard sweet tubes and packets; lollipop sticks; cigarette boxes; washing-up liquid bottles; cocoa tins; jam jars; milk bottle tops; toilet roll tubes; newspaper; corrugated cardboard; oddments of material; dried goods such as rice or macaroni; cardboard stiffening from the packing of new shirts; cellophane; greaseproof paper; silver foil; throw-away plastic beakers; margarine and butter tubs; cornflake packets.

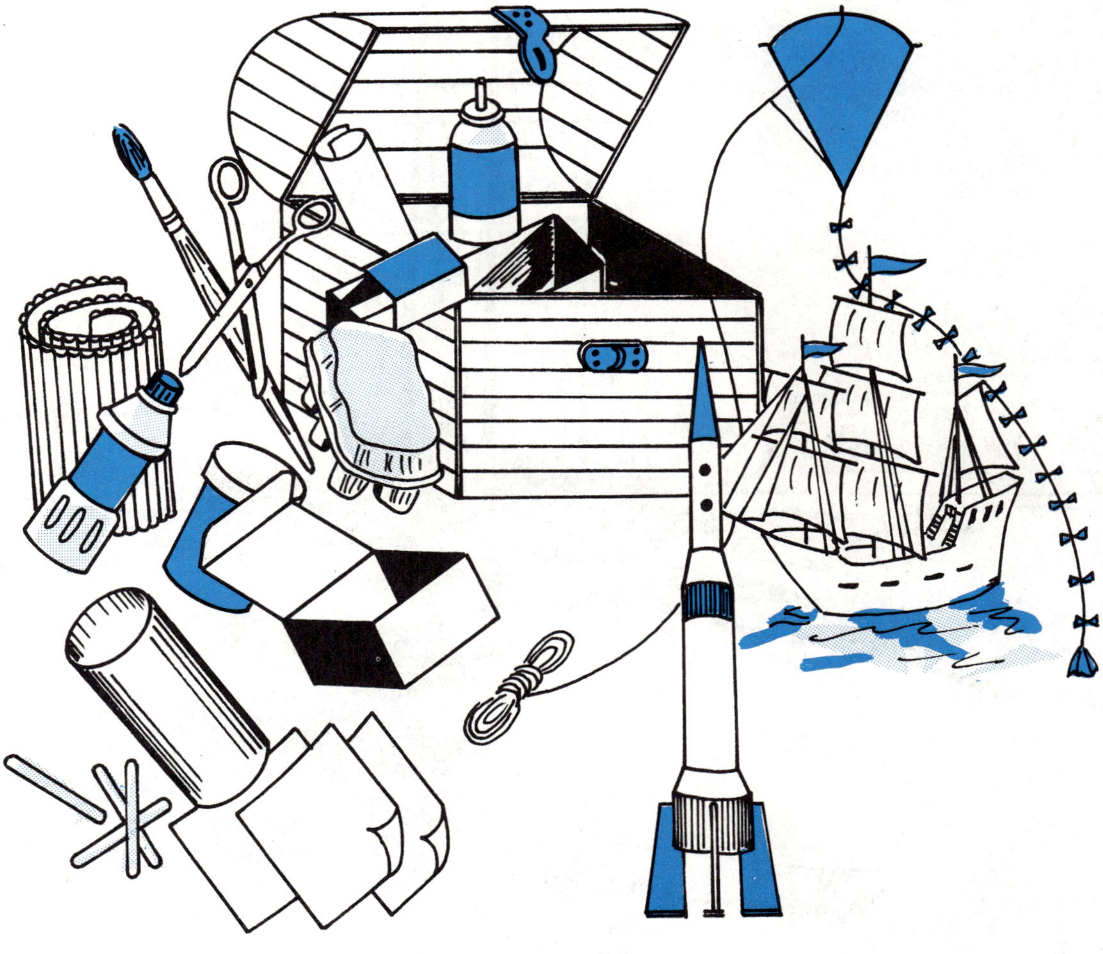

Voyage of Discovery

IN January 1915, the sailing ship *Endurance* was on course for the South Pole, making her way through the icy Weddell Sea and heading for Vahsel Bay. Aboard her the explorer Shackleton and his party were already feeling the effects of the sub-zero temperatures. Then the ship became caught in the drift of the current and was thrown off course, moving further and further away from her destination.
Finally the ice took hold and the *Endurance* was thrown almost onto her side. Shackleton realised that she would have to be abandoned.
The men made camp on the ice, taking the lifeboats with them. There they drifted onto the ice flow, waiting until the conditions would enable them to launch the boats.
All this time the party were soaked to the skin by the melting snow; and the breaking pack ice meant that the camp had to be constantly on the move.
The ice float slowly dwindled in size, until finally they had to launch the three boats.

The nearest land was now Elephant Island about one hundred miles away and the journey was a miserable one as gales constantly lashed the boats.
At last they landed upon the rocky coast, but Shackleton realised that they must get help before winter came upon them. Using only one of the boats he set sail with five of the men for the island of South Georgia, eight hundred miles away in one of the world's worst seas. There, he knew, they would find help on a whaling station.
Constantly they feared the boat would capsize, as the heavy seas tried to swamp them, but eventually after many trials and tribulations they reached the shore of the island—only to find that they had landed at the opposite end of the island to the whaling station!

They disembarked and made their first journey across the mountains in only thirty-six hours. They sighted the station and were soon able to reach civilisation and procure a boat to rescue the rest of the crew from Elephant Island.
So the terrible ordeal was over—man had fought against the elements and won.

Now we are off on our Voyage of Discovery

The Captain welcomes everybody aboard.

The Pack divides into four groups each representing one of the following countries:

Elephantopia
Giraffrica
Bearvaria
Parrotasia.

Each group designs a flag for their country.

Equipment: *For each group:—a sheet of cartridge paper, roughly quarto size; paints or crayons.*

Passports

Equipment: *For each Cub:—pencil; paper—roughly 15 × 10 cm (6 × 4 in).*

Each Cub is given a pencil and paper. He is asked to draw the face of the boy to his right. When he has completed the drawing, he passes it to the Cub he has drawn.

Through Customs

The leader is the Customs Officer. The four groups line up in file order. On the starting signal the first Cub in each team races to the Customs Officer and shows his passport.
Points are given for the first Cub each time.

Check your Kit

Equipment: *Two kitbags with identical objects inside—shirt, pullover, belt, towel, hat, socks, scarf, shoes, etc.*

The Pack divides into two teams. In each team the Cubs number one, two, three, four, etc, When a number is called, the kitbag is passed to that boy in each team. The leader then asks for an item and the first Cub to find the correct object, wins a point for his team.

Know the Elements

Equipment: *Beanbag.*

The Pack sits in a circle and the leader stands in the centre. He throws the beanbag to a Cub and shouts *'Earth!', 'Water!'* or *'Air!'*
The Cub has to shout back straight away the name of an animal for 'Earth', the name of a fish or sea creature for 'Water', or the name of a bird for 'Air'.

Lifeboat Drill

Equipment: *Rubber lifebelt or a circle of rope for each team.*

The four groups line up in file order. On the starting signal the first Cub in each team puts on the lifebelt and races to the end of the hall and back, then passes the lifebelt to the second member of the team and so on, continuing until the last member of the team is back in his place with the lifebelt removed.

Now the first part of our voyage is over and here we are at our first country.

America

Collage

Equipment: *For each group—roll of old wallpaper; coloured paper; pieces of cloth; glue; scissors.*

Preparation: A collage is a collection of bits and pieces stuck onto a background to represent anything—a pattern, a picture . . . to give the Cubs an idea of early America collect pictures of the early settlers; Red Indians; the ships arriving from England and perhaps tell the Pack the story of Columbus discovering America.
Then ask each group to do a collage of early America.

Lassos

Equipment: *For each group:—rope rings and lengths of string for lassos; 6 washing-up liquid bottles.*

Preparation: Attach the lengths of string to the rope rings. Place the bottles in a line in front of each group.
The groups line up in file order and in turn each member of a group tries to lasso one of his team's bottles.

Africa

What Animal

Equipment: *For each Cub:—a small card; a pin.*

Preparation: Write the name of an animal on each card and pin it to the back of each Cub, without allowing them to see what they are.
The Cubs then go around asking each other questions, which can only be answered *'Yes'* or *'No'* to find out which animal they represent.
As soon as they discover this they rush to tell the leader.

Paint the Witch Doctor

Equipment: *For four Cubs:—sheet of cartridge paper; wool; paints; brushes; overalls.*

Each group picks a witch doctor, who puts on the overalls and sits in front of them. A sheet of cartridge paper is tied over his face with the wool and he tries to paint his face guided by the directions his group shout at him. The best face, wins a point for that group.
Each group can make their own.

Japan

Make a Kite

Equipment: *Cloth, crepe paper or wrapping paper 1 metre × 75 cm (3 ft 4 in × 2 ft 6 in); scissors; cane or balsa wood—two lengths 1 metre & 60 cm (3 ft 4 in & 2 ft); sheet of crepe paper; several elastic bands; ball of string; glue.*

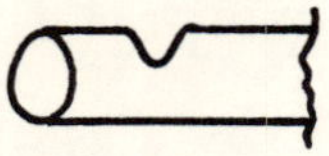

Notch end of canes

Lash two pieces of wood together as shown in the illustration. Join all the ends tightly with string.

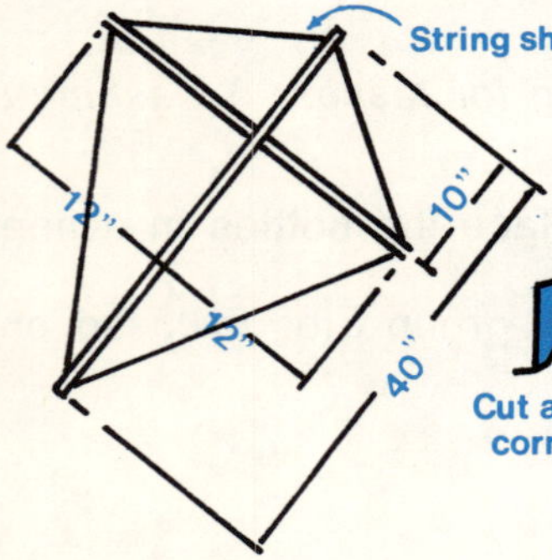

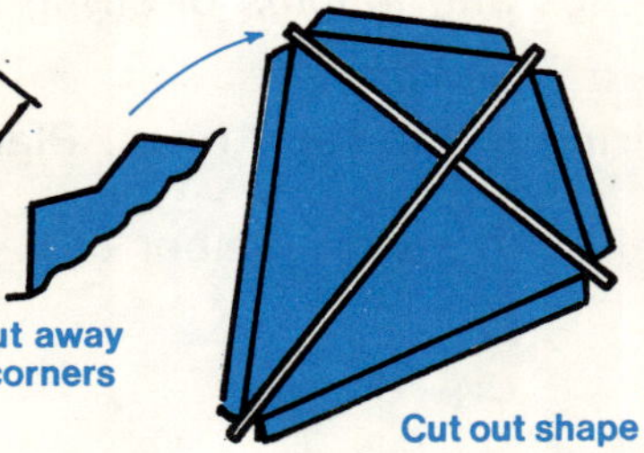

Cut the paper slightly wider than the frame. Fold the paper over the string and glue.

Attach the string as shown in the diagram, fixing the elastic band.

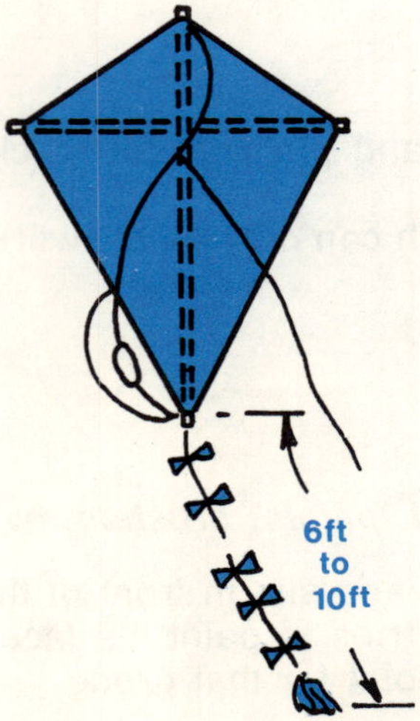

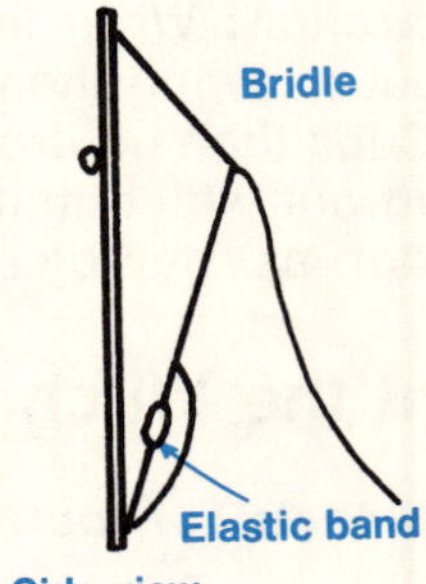

Side view

Make bows out of the crepe paper and tie these to the string to make a trailer.

You can make all sorts of kites as these pictures show. Try to design a new one.

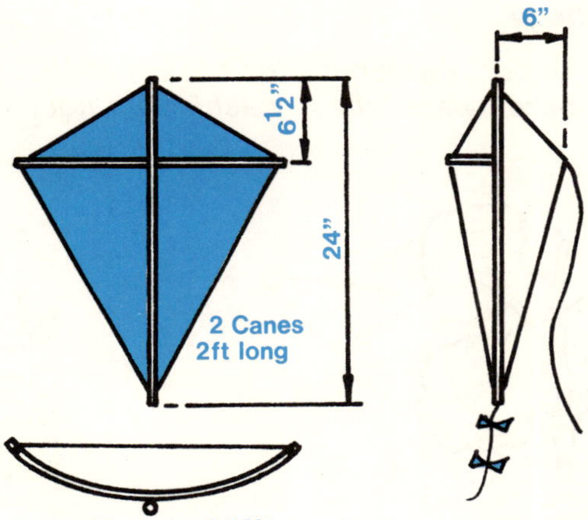

Bow Fronted Kite

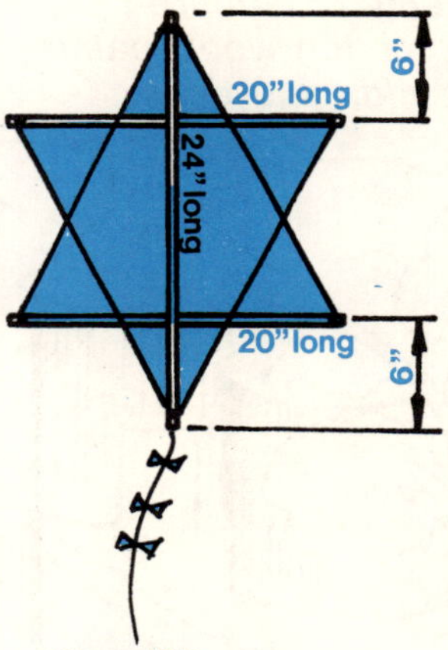

Star Kite

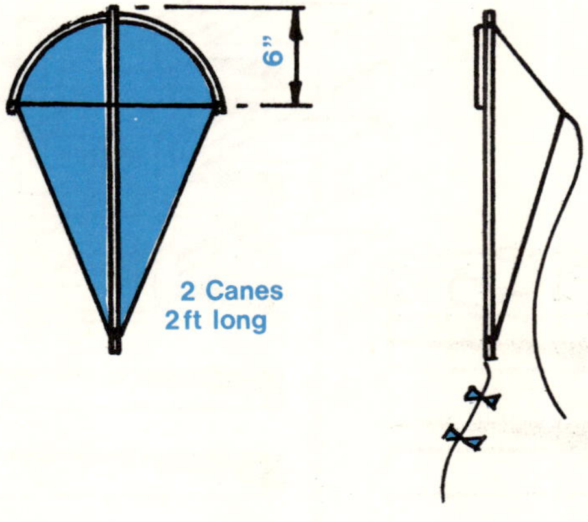

English Bow Top Kite

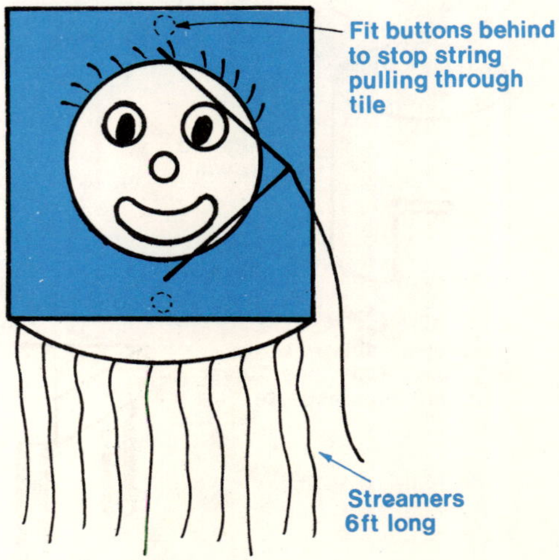

Tile Kite

Around the World

Each group makes one of the following: **An African Village**
An American City
An Eskimo Village
An Arab Village.

Equipment: *Plenty of coloured paper and cartridge paper; cardboard for bases; string; cotton; glue; scissors; cotton wool; paints; crayons; cardboard sweet tubes; washing-up liquid bottles and any other odds and ends.*

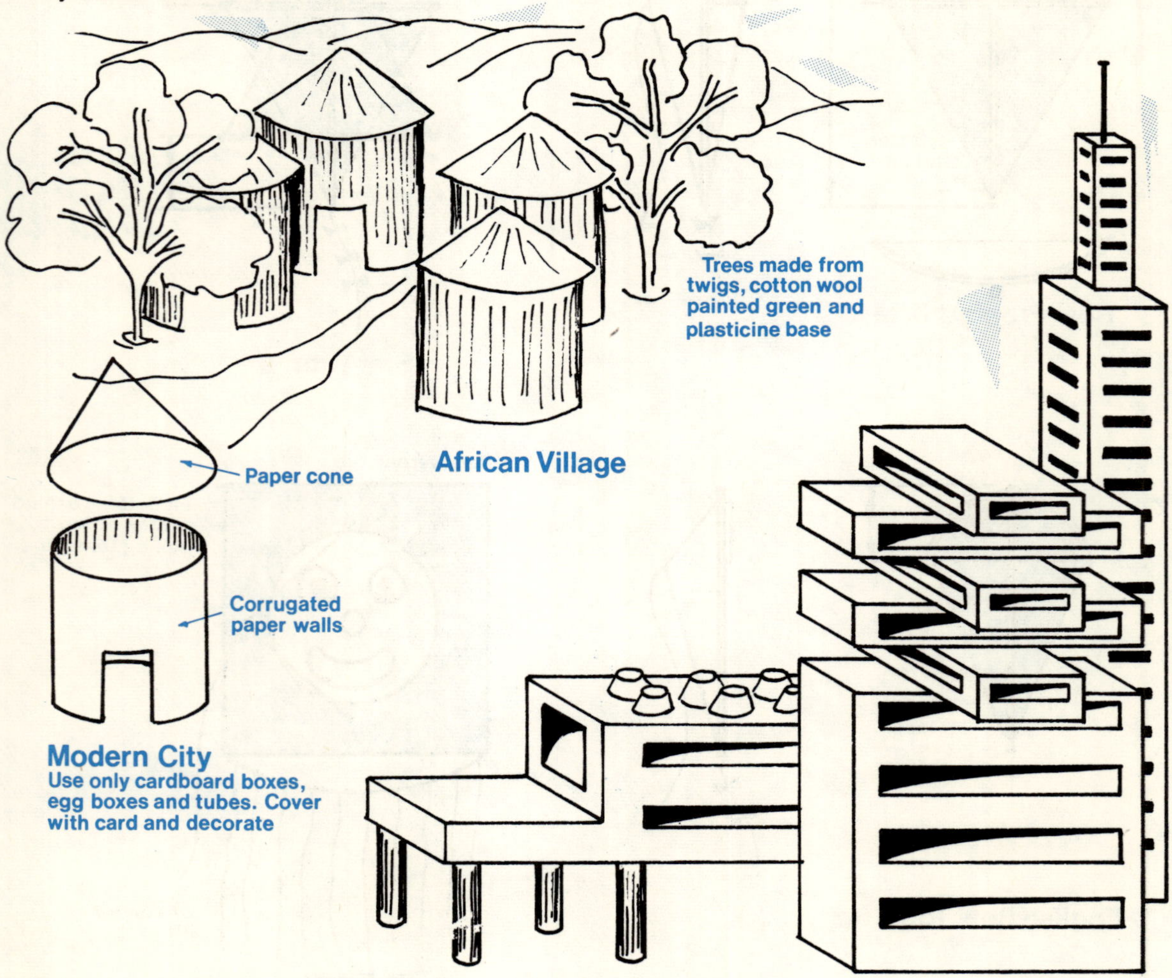

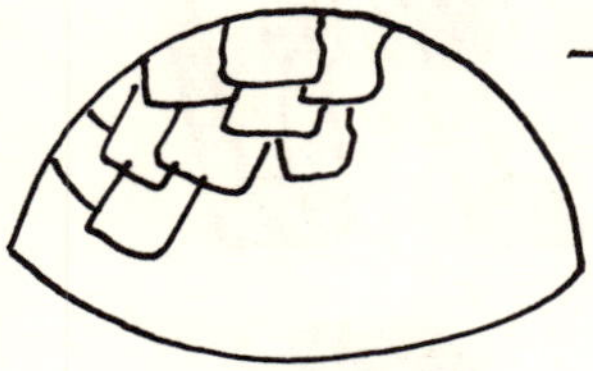

Old tennis ball cut in half (alternative plasticine) Cover with several layers of paper. Allow to dry, remove ball

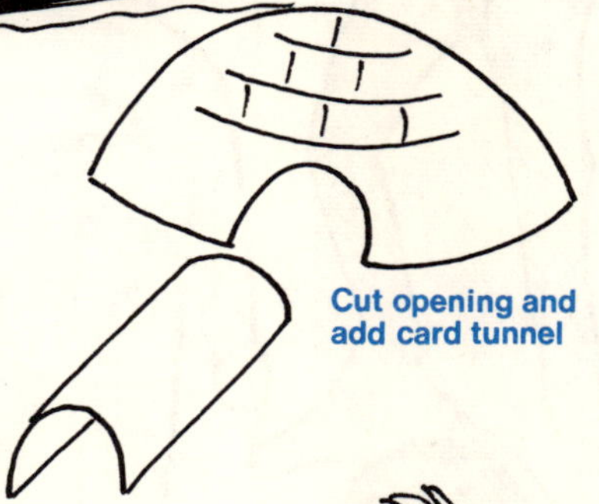

Cut opening and add card tunnel

Bible Houses

1 Cut card to fit top of box
2 Fit card sides allowing extra height for parapet
3 Cut stairs from balsa wood
4 Paint doorways and windows

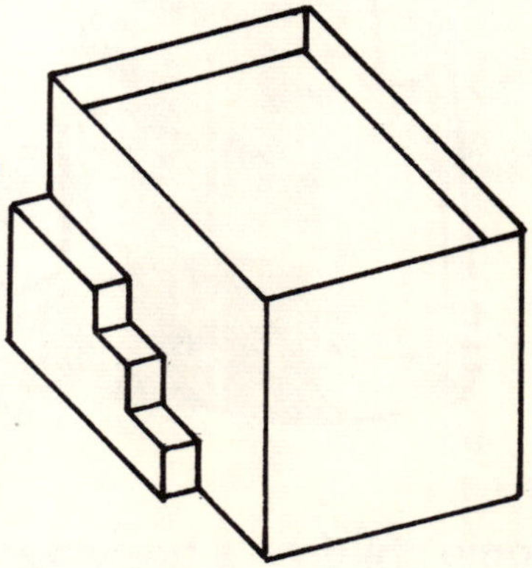

Palm Trees

Straw trunk with pipe cleaner wound spiral fashion. Paint brown. Fit green paper leaves and plasticine base

 Here are some children's drawings of people around the world.

Passing the Coral Stone

Equipment: *Stone or pebble for each team; chalk.*

The Pack divides into two teams which line up in file order. A chalk goal line is drawn across the centre of the hall.
On the starting signal each leader passes a stone to any member of his team without the other team seeing who it is passed to. Then team A guesses where team B's stone is. If they are correct, they can take a pace forward; if they are wrong, then the other team steps forward.
Team A now try to hide the stone themselves and team B guess where it is. The first team to reach the centre line, scores a goal.

Market Place

Equipment: *Sign for each shop; posters if possible; a list of badge requirements for each group; paper for money; pencils.*

Chemist—*Health*
Sports Shop—*Feats of Skill*
Police Station—*Exploring*
Town Park—*Discovering Nature*
Secondhand Shop—*Safety*
Dry Cleaners—*Service*
Travel Agents—*Flags and Countries*
Driving School—*Safety*
Hardware Store—*Handcraft*
Theatre—*Entertaining*
Post Office—*Knotting*
Town Hall—*Promise and Law.*

Each group sends a member to one of the above shops to pass a test. The shopkeeper will then give a note of the change out of 10p for each item, depending on how well the Cub does.

Spot the Country

Equipment: *For each group: 10 cards; paper and pencils.*

Preparation: Write the name of a country, jumbled up, on each card. The first group to hand in a correct list of the countries to the leader wins.

United Nations

Equipment: *One large and one small set of 12 cards.*

Preparation: Write the name of a country on each large card and duplicate the sets. Place the large cards around the hall and keep the small ones.
The Cubs run around the hall until the leader calls *'Land'* when they land in one of the countries by standing near a card. The leader then picks one of the small cards and calls out the name of a country. The Cubs already standing in that country then gain a point for their group.
The group with the lowest score at the end wins.

Travelling for Adventure

THE flight of the Vulcan bomber of 44 Squadron, R.A.F. was a routine low-level check. Flight Lieutenant Alcock was checking the instruments and finding everything normal, it was just an ordinary flight. The crew were happy and relaxed.

It was not until they began to climb that trouble started. A loud explosion made Alcock turn and look behind him. Number one engine was on fire. Seconds later the spreading flames caught number two engine alight.

The aircraft continued to climb and the crew put out both fires. This was only a momentary respite, for as they continued to climb, it was noticed that the underside of the wing was now burning fiercely.

It now became obvious that the aircraft would have to be abandoned. Quickly Flight Lieutenant Alcock ordered the crew to eject. Now he was alone.

The aircraft was a ball of flame, but looking earthwards he noticed that he was still over a densely populated area.
With great coolness he guided the aircraft away from the built-up area. The many minutes that passed must have seemed like an eternity, but at last he was over open ground, and he finally ejected.
The plane crashed in an open space and the town's people were saved from disaster by one man's coolness.
Flight Lieutenant Alcock was awarded the Air Force Cross for his great heroism.

Make a model glider, like the one in this picture.

Glider

Equipment: *A sheet of thick cardboard or thin balsa wood, roughly 2·5 x 20·3 cm (1 x 8 in); a sheet of thin cardboard 22·8 cm (9 in) square; glue; elastic band; small stick, roughly 15·2 cm (6 in)—for launching; model or craft knife.*

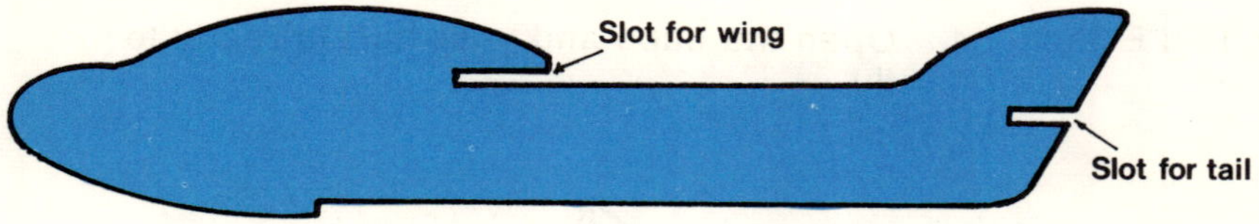

Cut out the shape from the balsa wood, as shown in the diagram.

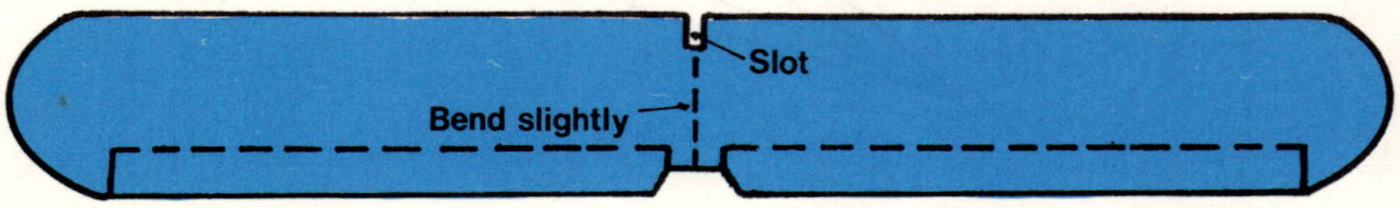

Now cut out the wings from the thin cardboard.

Take care to cut the tail correctly.

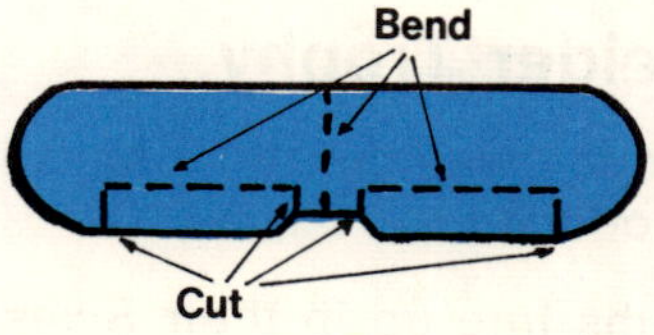

Now glue the parts together.
Fit the elastic band to the stick and launch the glider.

Paper Darts

Equipment: *1 sheet of foolscap paper.*

1. Fold the paper in half, lengthways. Then open it up again and fold A to A and B to B.

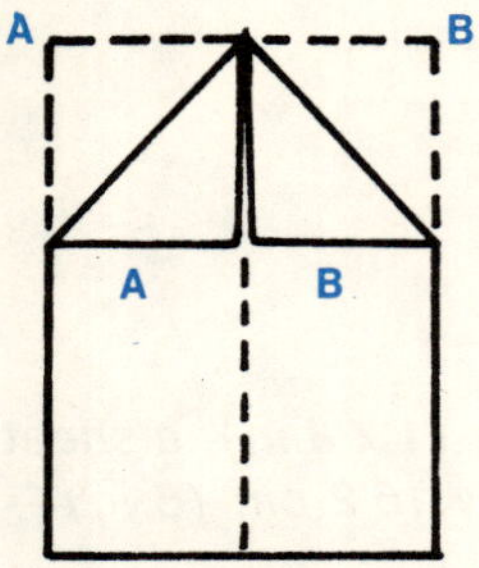

2. Fold C to C and D to D.

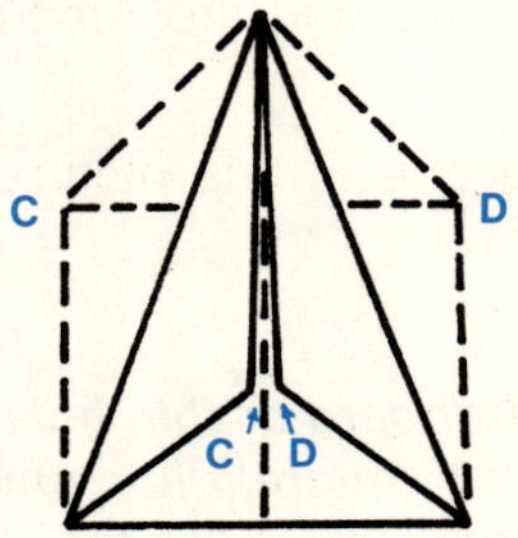

3. Fold the dart in half and then fold E to F on both sides.

4. Open the flaps and your dart is ready to fly.

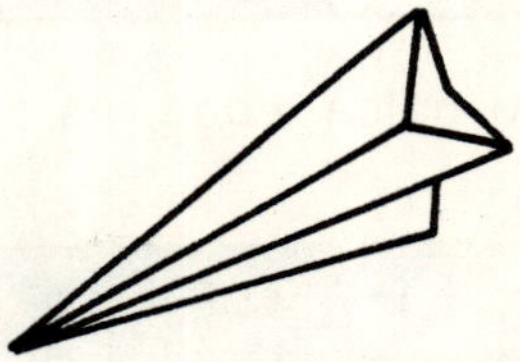

Schneider Trophy

This trophy was the prize for an air race in the 1930's, out of which the forerunner of the Spitfire was produced.

The Cubs line up in their Sixes in file order.
The aim of each team is to see who can fly their paper darts for the longest distance. A system of points could be devised—five points for the longest flight, three points for the second and one point for the third. When all the Cubs have flown their darts, the total score for each team can be added up to find the winner.
Alternatively the flight of the gliders can be judged in much the same way, but on performance rather than distance flown.

Handcraft Projects

Helicopters

Equipment: *Sheet of cartridge paper 15·2 cm (6 in) square; thick card 15·2 × 2·5 cm (6 × 1 in); long pin; glue; scissors.*

Cut a 15·2 cm (6 in) square of paper as shown in the picture.

From each corner cut diagonally, nearly to the centre.

Fold the tour corners to the centre and glue.

Cut a strip of card—thick enough to put a pin into.

Fit the pin through the centre of the rotor and into the card, so that the rotor spins freely.
Drop the helicopter from a reasonable height and the rotor will spin.

Jet Boat

Equipment: *Sheet of balsa wood approximately 20·3 × 15·2 cm (8 × 6 in); coping saw; cigar tube; 4 pins; small piece of candle; small sheet of cardboard roughly 7·6 cm (3 in) square; matches.*

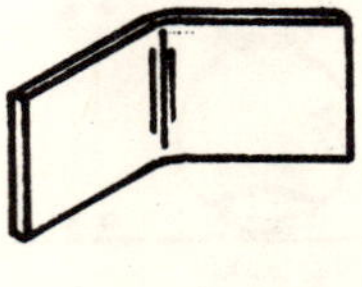

Cut the sheet of balsa wood to a point at the front and cut a piece of card in the shape of a rudder as shown in the diagram.

Cross two large pins and push these into the balsa wood at either end of the boat to hold the cigar tube.

In the cap of the cigar tube make a small hole, as close to the centre of the cap as possible.

Fix the candle firmly to the balsa wood under the middle of the tube. Put some water in the tube and replace the cap. Place the tube on the pin cradles and the boat in a bowl of water. Then light the candle. When the water becomes hot, steam will be produced and will force its way out of the hole in the cap, pushing the jet boat along.

Optical Illusions

The eyes can be deceived, not only by distance but by the speed at which objects move.
For instance, try the Goldfish Bowl:

Equipment: *Thin sheet of cardboard, roughly 20·3 × 30 cm (8 × 12 in); pencils; short length of string.*

Draw a goldfish bowl on one side of the card and a fish on the opposite side, as shown in the diagram.

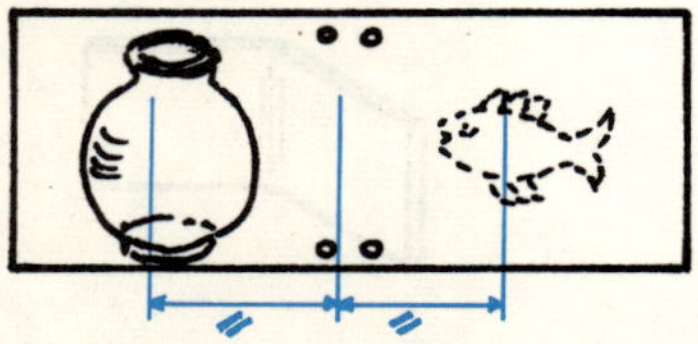

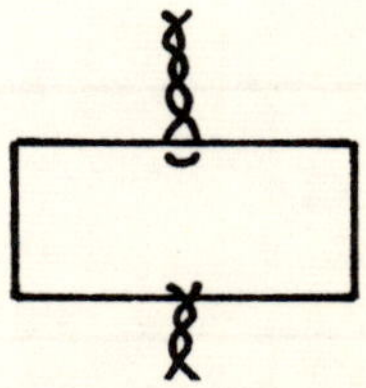

Fit a piece of string top and bottom of the card as shown. Wind the string and then pull tight. The card will spin and the fish will appear to be in the bowl.

If you are still not convinced, try another test:

Equipment: *Thin cardboard sheet approximately 20·3 × 30 cm (8 × 12 in); pencils.*

Draw a birdcage on the card and then, a short distance away, a bird. Hold the card at arm's length, then slowly move it towards your eyes. When the card is close, the bird will seem to move into the cage.

Games

Monte Carlo Rally

The Pack divides into four or more teams. Each team stands in single file like the spokes of a wheel, with the team leaders at the rim. All the Cubs face outwards from the centre.
Two chairs are positioned in front of each leader, approximately four feet apart. These are the entrances to the pits and the outside circle is the race track.
On the starting signal, the leaders race out from the pits and run round the track in a clockwise direction. As soon as they are back in place the next Cub in the team can race.
When every Cub in the team has run then the whole team run together for a lap of honour. Any boy who touches the entrance to any pit must start again.

Yes-No

Preparation: A list of questions on the Highway Code which can only be answered by *'Yes'* or *'No'*. Two signs reading Yes and No. The Sixes line up in file order in the centre of the hall and are numbered off. One chair is placed at either end of the hall, one bearing the *'Yes'* sign and the other the *'No'* sign.

The leader starts by asking the first boy in each Six a question from his list—e.g. *'Does amber follow green in traffic lights?'—'Can a policeman direct you across the road?'—'Should you cross the road from behind a parked car?'—'Should you ride your cycle when it has faulty brakes?'—'Should you ride your cycle if your feet do not touch the ground when it is stationary?'—'In a busy street, which also has traffic lights at a junction would you cross the road anywhere?'*
The Cubs run to either the *'Yes'* or *'No'* chairs. The first Cub to sit on the correct chair, wins a point for his Six. The leader then asks the 'No. 2' boys in each Six a question and so on.

Shunting

The Pack divides into equal teams and lines up in file order. The leaders of the teams are railway engines and the rest of the team is the train. The trains all stand at one end of the hall. On the starting signal the engine races to the other end of the hall, touches the wall and shunts (runs backwards) back to his team as fast as he can. He picks up the first carriage and repeats the performance until the whole train is pulled to the end of the hall and shunted back to the start.

Project Treasure

THE ancient Inca civilisation in South America thought nothing of their natural riches, although gold and precious jewels were in abundance.

It was not until the arrival of the Spanish Conquistadors that any importance was attached to the wealth. But very soon mule trains were carrying the new-found treasure through the jungle paths to the Spanish fleet anchored in the bay.

The jubilant Spaniards bore off the treasure in their ships, but their success was short-lived, Sir Francis Drake and the English fleet lay in ambush. Very soon guns were being run out and broadside after broadside raked the Spanish ships. Boarding parties were soon transferring the treasure to the English vessels.

But misfortune swiftly befell the English also. A hurricane swept one of the ships onto a coral reef where she sunk with her treasure.

Nothing more was heard of the hidden treasure for many years, until that famous pirate Blackbeard discovered the remains of the ship and with it the treasure.

But Blackbeard too had enemies, and the worst of these, Captain Henry Morgan, sent out spies to find him. They reported to Morgan that Blackbeard was heading for Maricaibo Bay.

As the ships entered the Bay Morgan's vessels fired powerful broadsides and before the boarding parties could reach the crippled ships, they sank—committing the treasures once again to the ocean bed.

For many years divers searched without success, until a party of American archaeologists finally discovered its location. Natives had found the riches and taken them to decorate their temple in the jungle.

The party boarded their 'plane with the glad news, to return to the United States but like so many discoverers of the ill-fated treasure they were doomed to lose their lives. The 'plane crashed into the jungle and not one lived to tell the tale of where they had found the treasure.

Action Projects

In Search of the Treasure

Equipment: *Set of postcards, paper and pencil for each Cub.*

Preparation: Make a set of cards as follows:

London 0900 hrs.
Lisbon 1000 hrs.

Algiers 1200 hrs.
Ghana 1400 hrs.

Florida 2015 hrs.
Santa-Fe 2210 hrs.

Dallas 2350 hrs.
Mexico 2400 hrs.

Lisbon 1000 hrs.
Algiers 1200 hrs.

Ghana 1400 hrs.
Florida 2015 hrs.

Santa-Fe 2210 hrs.
Dallas 2350 hrs.

Mexico 2400 hrs.
South America 0115 hrs.

Spread these cards around the hall.
The Cubs are organised into teams, each representing a different country—i.e. America, Holland, France, Belgium, Norway, Russia etc.
They are told the name of the starting airport and the final destination. Then they must find the cards (London leads to Lisbon etc.) and make a note of all the airports and the times. On arrival in South America the times are changed into the twelve hour clock.

Setting up Base

Equipment: *For each team—timber base a suitable offcut; garden cane approximately 1·50 m (5 ft) high; ball of string; two sheets of cartridge paper; paints or crayons; hand drill; hammer and nails; paper 30 x 15 cm (12 x 6 in); sticky tape; tape measure.*

Flagstaff

1. One of the Cubs colours or paints the flag of his team's country on the cartridge paper, he then folds over one end of the flag and is ready with the sticky tape to fix the flag to the pole.
2. Another Cub drills a hole in the centre of the flag base, measuring the exact point with the tape measure. The hole must allow the garden cane to fit exactly into the base.
3. A third Cub cuts a length of string to support the flagstaff.
4. A fourth Cub is ready with the hammer and nails, and he bangs a nail down in each corner of the base to act as a peg for the guy lines.

The first fixes the flag to the end of the cane and the Cubs then fix this in the base. While one of them holds the pole the others attach the string round the pole with guy lines out to the four corners of the base. The fourth Cub now makes a loop with the end of each line and secures it round the nail so that the flagstaff is firmly supported.

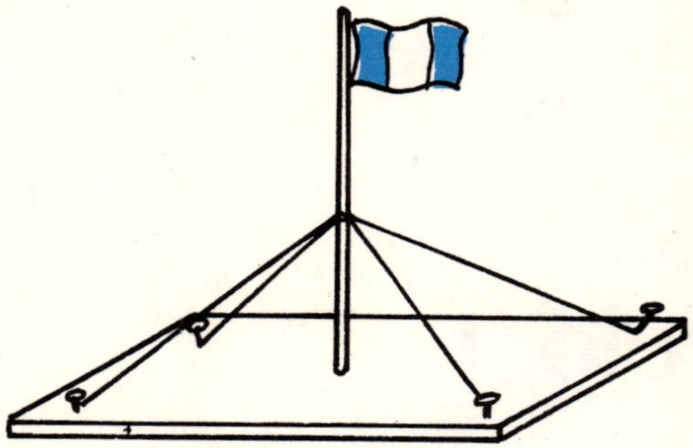

Tents

Each team takes its sheet of paper and folds it, as shown in the diagram to make a tent.

1. Fold the sheet of paper in half.

2. Fold in each end.

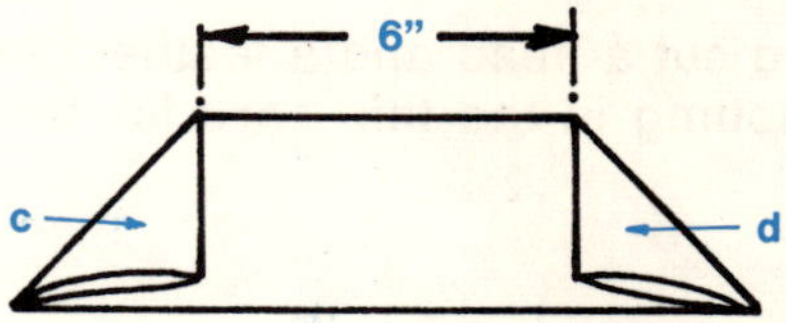

3. Reverse and fold in c and d.

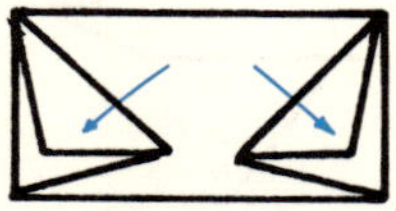

4. Open up and push ends inwards.

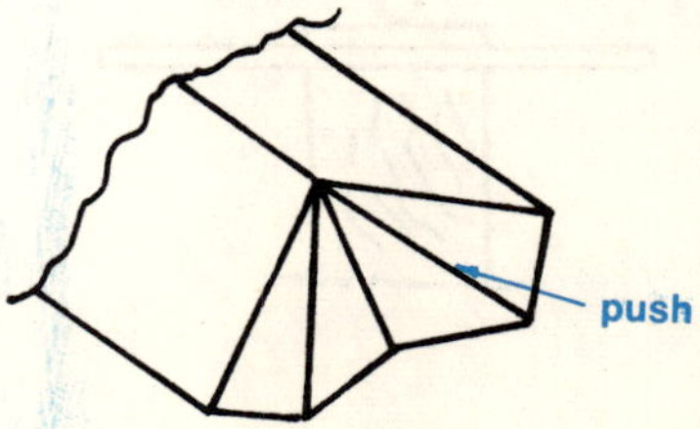

5. Fold bottom point under. Glue or stick together with tape.

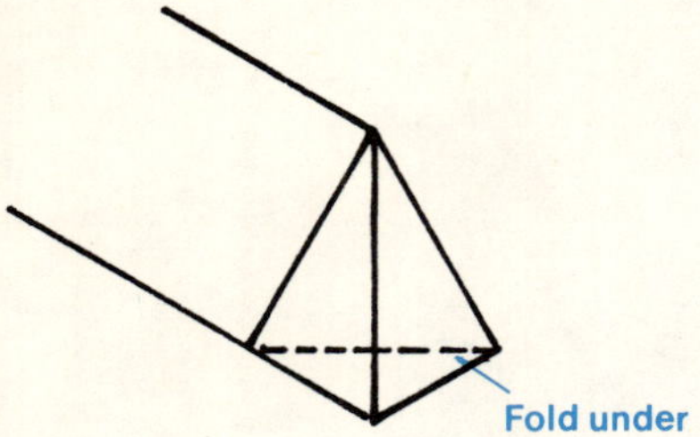

6. Tent.

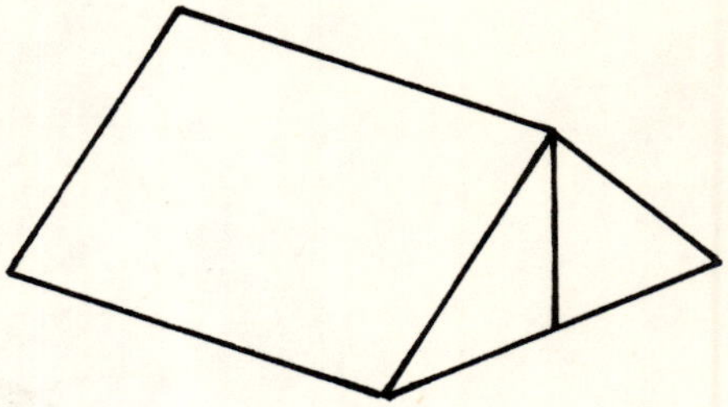

Handcraft Project

Weather Station

Make a weather vane to show the direction of the wind before setting out on your journey to find the treasure.

Equipment: *For each team—2·5 cm (1 in) wide card; thin card for the pointer and the compass cards; a nail; 2 threading beads; 15 cm (6 in) length of timber fixed to the ground or block of wood; hammer; felt-tipped pen.*

Out of the wide card cut a head and a feather, for either end of the pointer like an arrow. Then slit each end for slotting in the thin card for the pointer.

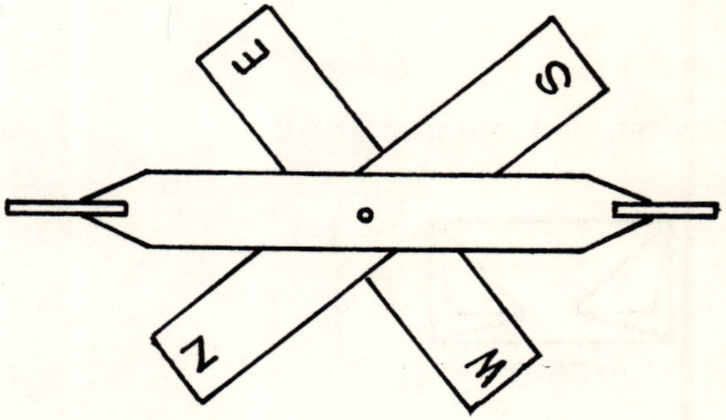

Make compass cards and mark them with the points of the compass in bold lettering—N.S.E.W. Make a hole in the centre of the pointer and the compass cards, placing the beads in between. Put the whole weather vane on top of the wooden post and hammer the nail into place.

Games

Jungle Trail

Before you can set out to find the treasure you must frighten off all the wild animals.

Equipment: *Coloured wool for armbands—red, brown, yellow, green, blue.*

The Pack splits into two groups. One group represents animals and have coloured armbands:

Mountain Lion	**red**	**10 points**
Monkey	**brown**	**5 points**
Deer	**yellow**	**2 points**
Alligator	**green**	**8 points**
Snake	**blue**	**7 points**

All the animals hide. The second team sets out to hunt the animals and can capture them by taking their armbands.
Each captured animal can collect a new armband from the leader and rejoin the game.
After a suitable period of time, the sides change places and a record is kept of scores.

Find the Treasure

Now that a base camp has been established and all the jungle animals frightened away, the explorers should be ready to start out to find the treasure.
Four messages have been given to each team during the programme. All the messages are in code, but only one is decipherable—and this gives the location of the treasure.

Equipment: *A set of four messages on cards for each team; a code for each team; a box of treasure.*

Suggested code:

A	B	C	D	E	F	G	H	I	J	K	L	M	N	O	P	Q	R	S	T	U	V	W	X	Y	Z
V	**W**	**X**	**Y**	**Z**	**A**	**B**	**C**	**D**	**E**	**F**	**G**	**H**	**I**	**J**	**K**	**L**	**M**	**N**	**O**	**P**	**Q**	**R**	**S**	**T**	**U**

Once the teams are given the code they can start deciphering the messages and when they find the right one they rush to find the concealed treasure which can be hidden anywhere nearby.

Journey into Space

TEN, nine, eight, seven, six, five, four, three, two, one, zero, blast off!'*

After an ideal blast off, the voyage to the moon was proceeding with perfection. The astronauts relaxed and tried to get as much rest as possible before the busy time ahead. Two days had passed and the earth had dwindled to a small sphere. Commander James Lovell and Fred Haise had entered Aquarius (the lunar module) and tested the systems in preparation for the moon landing. John Swigert was listening to instructions from Mission Control for photographing a comet known as 'Bennett.'

Swigert replied *'Okay stand by'* and after a brief pause *'Okay Houston. Hey, we've got a problem here.'*

'This is Houston. Say again please.'

Swigert repeated *'Houston, we've got a problem.'*

Red and yellow lights began blinking inside the spacecraft and on the panels at Mission Control.

Swigert calmly added: *'We've had a pretty large bang.'*

Oxygen tank number two had ruptured. The oxygen was spilling out. Lovell looked out of the window and saw vapour streaming by. Oxygen tank number one was now leaking through a valve. Mission Control told the astronauts to think about using the lunar module as a lifeboat.

The lunar module, designed for landing two men on the moon, would now have to become the living quarters. Would there be enough oxygen, chemicals to clean the atmosphere, electricity to operate the water to cool the systems?
The lunar module would have to provide propulsion until just before re-entry into the atmosphere.
The astronauts transferred the guidance information from the command module's computer to the lunar module. Lovell called the transfer *'our first milestone'*.
Without any words from the astronauts or Mission Control it was obvious that any attempt to land on the moon would have to be abandoned.
Would it be possible to bring the astronauts back to earth alive?
It was decided by discussion between Mission Control and the astronauts to allow the craft to move on its natural course around the moon, and then with far less expenditure of energy, to give a slight push that would bring it under the earth's attraction.
With precise tracking information from Mission Control the astronauts managed a perfect course correction.
Emerging from behind the moon the astronauts fired the craft's engines to accelerate their return to earth.
Tracking now showed that the acceleration burn had somehow placed the craft on a course that would take it within 100 miles of the earth and the craft would bounce off the atmosphere. A mid-course correction would be needed.
Using the dividing line between night and day, and the sun as reference points the astronauts would be able to align their craft precisely. With computers Mission Control calculated the degrees of angle needed.
As Lovell swivelled the craft to the angle, the sun came shining through the window at exactly the position predicted.
Another serious problem had to be overcome, their breathing was adding carbon dioxide to the craft's atmosphere.
Mission Control worked out *'Your friendly Do-It-Yourself Kit.'* With sticky tape the astronauts pasted cardboard around the sides of the command module canisters, so that they could be rigged to the landing vehicle system. It worked.
The last hurdle was to dispose of the damaged service module and lunar module. With a push-pull manoevre they pulled away from the service module. As it floated away they saw the damage. *'It's a real mess',* reported Lovell.
They now entered the command module, and pushed the lunar module away. Mission Control said *'Farewell, Aquarius, and we thank you.'*
The command module was now falling towards earth at a speed of 25,000 miles an hour.
On contact with the atmosphere, friction gradually slowed the craft down. For three minutes radio communication was interrupted.
Then voices could be heard. They were on their way home.
The parachutes unfurled, and they landed in the sea. The fantastic journey was over.
Three men, with great courage, and hundreds of people at Mission Control, had matched their wits against the vastness of space, and had won.

Adapted from the report of Apollo 13 by **Walter Froelich.**

Games

Weather Station

Equipment: *Set of cards for each Six; glue; cotton wool; a blue crayon.*
Preparation: Colour each card blue and then paste some cotton wool cloud onto each in a different cloud formation, e.g. cumulus, stratus.
The Sixes line up in relay formation and each Cub runs forward as the leader calls out the name of a cloud formation. The Cub picks up the appropriate card and races with it to the leader.

U.F.O.'s

Equipment: *Paper plate for each Cub.*

The Cubs line up in relay formation and each Cub tries to throw his Sixes' plate as far as possible. The team to get the highest score of 'long shots' is the winner.

Land on the Moon

Equipment: *Football.*

The Pack divides into two teams and forms circles at opposite ends of the room. One circle represents the moon and the other, the earth.
The leader stands in the centre of the earth circle and throws the ball to each Cub in turn.
Meanwhile the first Cub in the moon team, races around the earth and back to his circle. When all the Cubs in that team have been in orbit, the last Cub shouts 'Landed' and the leader stops throwing the ball. He makes a record of the earth team's score of correct catches and the teams reverse.
The team landing during the lowest catch score is the winner.

Lunar Module leaves Moon

Equipment: *For each Six—jam jar; ping pong ball.*
The Sixes line up in relay formation. Each Cub in turn races to the end of the hall and back holding the jam jar, containing the ping pong ball, upside down. He keeps the ball from falling out, by rotating the jar.

Splashdown

Equipment· *1 length of rope for each Six.*
The Sixes line up in relay formation, with the Sixers standing at the opposite end of the hall facing them. Each Sixer is a helicopter and he races to the first member of his Six, who are spacemen, ties the rope around his waist with a bowline and winches him in. This is continued until all the spacemen are transferred to the other end of the hall.

Action Projects

Star Viewer

Equipment: *Pencil; pin. For each Cub—a cardboard tube, e.g. a toilet roll; a piece of thin square card.*

Preparation: Mark on each card the size of the end of the tube and then draw a star constellation within that circle and pinprick all the stars.

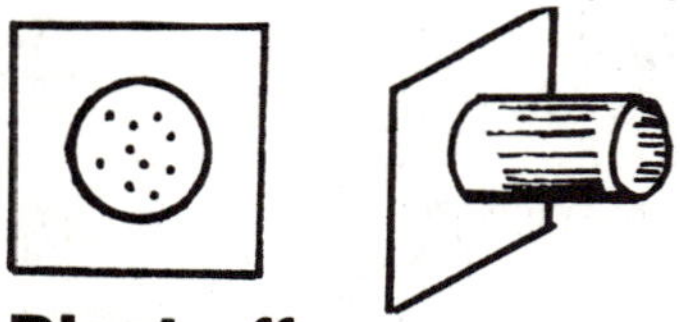

Each Cub has a tube, he collects a card and views the constellation through his telescope by holding the card to the light.

Blast off

Equipment: *For each Six—a number of sausage shaped balloons; a ball of string; sheet of paper, approx. quarto size; sticky tape; couple of paper clips.*

Preparation: Blow up the balloon. Make a paper dart and attach it with sticky tape to the balloon. Fix two paper clips to the paper dart and thread a length of string through these.

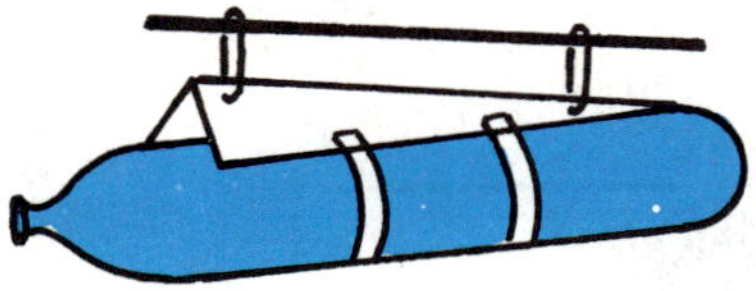

One boy holds one end of the string and another holds the other end and the neck of the balloon.
The balloon is released so that the air escapes and propels the rocket along the string.

3-D Viewer

Equipment: *Cardboard, approx. 15 cm (6 in) square; ruler; scissors.*

Preparation: Draw a cross on the cardboard, 5 cm (2 in) square, the width of each part being 1·25 cm ($\frac{1}{2}$ in). Cut this out.

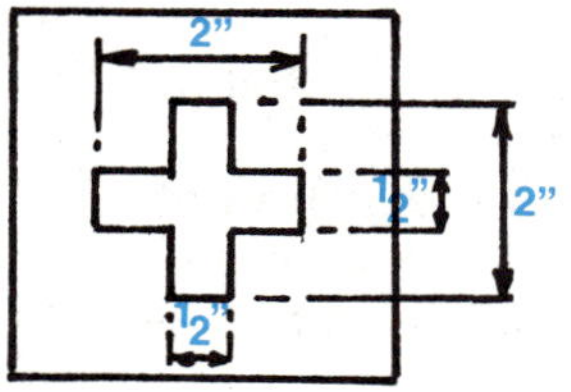

Stand the card at right angles to a picture and look through the cross; after a minute the picture, especially if it has buildings in it, looks three-dimensional.

Handcraft Projects

Each Six makes the following—**Lunar Landscape**
Robot
Space Rocket

Lunar Landscape

Equipment: *Hardboard base; cardboard box; cheese boxes; old cloth; newspaper; plaster of paris; sheet of card for background; emery cloth; paste; scissors; paper.*

1. Paste the cheese boxes onto the hardboard base and cut out the cardboard box as shown in the diagram.

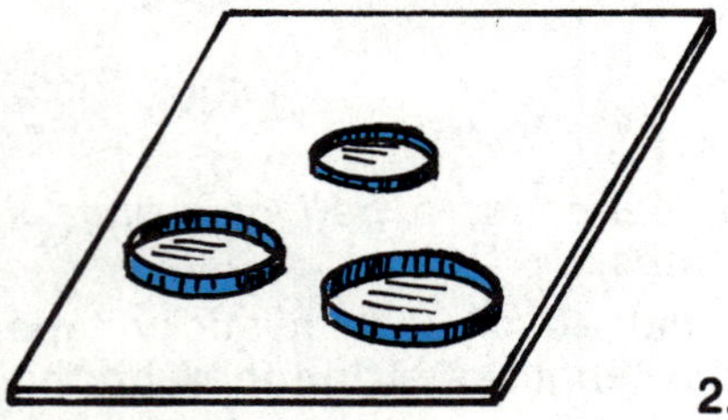

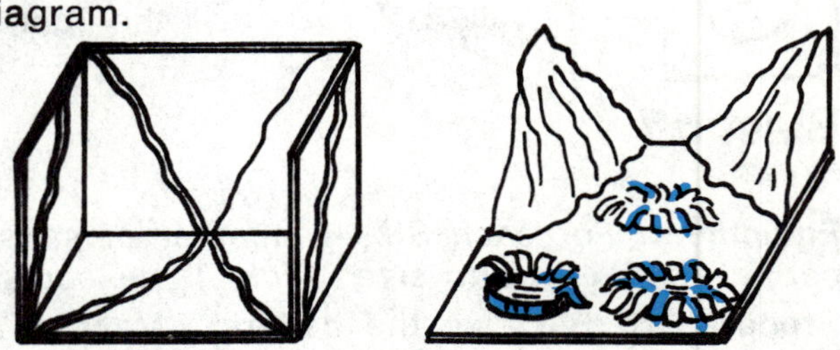

2. Cover the cut-up box with cloth and the cheese boxes with strips of paper.

3. Pour the mixed plaster of paris over the model.

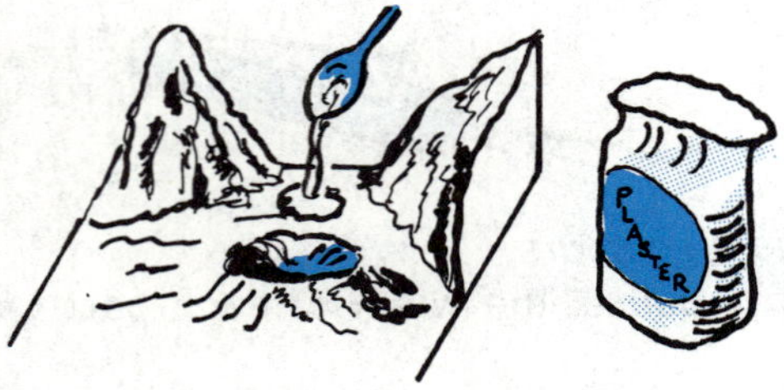

4. Paint a cardboard background, fix it up behind the model and cover it with emery cloth.

Guidelines: The hardboard can be any size—e.g. 1 metre (1 yd) square and it can be obtained from a local timber merchant, together with the emery cloth, which is rather like sandpaper.
The cardboard box could be a shoebox, as these are made from thin cardboard and are easy to cut. The cheese boxes referred to are the circular variety.

Robot

Equipment: *Boxes of various shapes and sizes; plastic egg box; old buttons; coloured gummed paper; strong adhesive; split pins; scissors.*

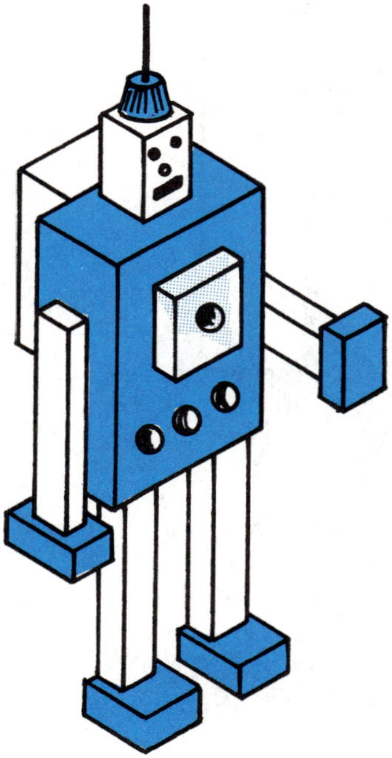

1. Form the robot as shown in the diagram. Start with the legs and feet. Two square boxes can be used for the feet and covered in gummed paper. The legs can be biscuit boxes or toothpaste tube boxes, and these can be covered in gummed paper and stuck onto the feet.
2. The body can be a cornflake packet or a soap powder box, covered in gummed paper and with buttons stuck on to represent the knobs on the control panel.
3. For the arms, pierce holes in the sides of the body, open the top of the box or packet and poke a split pin outwards through each hole, bending the two spikes so that they do not fall out.
4. Attach two toothpaste tube packets on either side, by piercing the side of each packet with the split pin, by straightening the spikes to pierce a hole, then opening the top of the packet and bending the spikes inside it. Now the arms will swing.
5. Paste matchboxes onto the ends of the arms as hands.
6. Seal up the end of the body and stick another square box on top for the head. Cut out one of the egg box compartments and stick it on top as a helmet with a stick coming from it like an aerial.
7. Eyes, nose and mouth can be made from buttons.

Rocket

Equipment: *Cardboard tube or plastic bottles; smaller cardboard tube; thin card; paper; length of dowelling; matchsticks.*

Guidelines: The plastic bottle can easily be a washing-up liquid container. The smaller cardboard tube may be a sweets tube. Dowelling is thin wooden rod and may be obtained from your local timber yard.

1. Cut out a large circle of thin card, at least 2·5 cm (1 in) in diameter, larger than the main tube. Then cut away a segment of this.
   This will provide the cone.
2. Cut four fins from the cardboard and attach some thin dowelling to the end of each—like this—

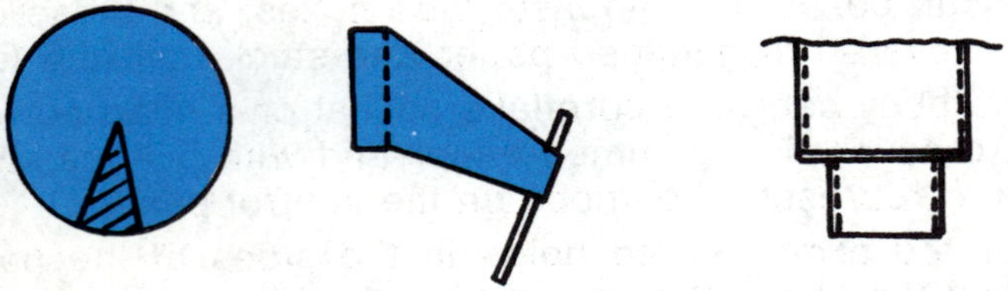

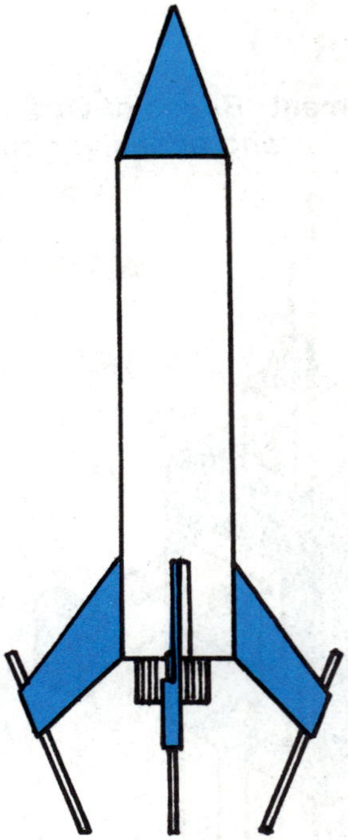

3. Glue the smaller tube to the main tube and cover it with matchsticks.

Some more things to make:

Egg Box Martian

Equipment: *A cardboard egg box; thin card; paints; glue; scissors.*

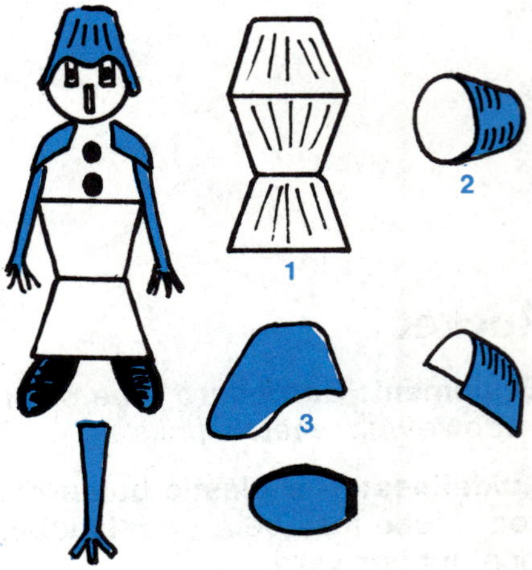

1. Cut out three egg box compartments and glue them together like this—
2. Cut out another compartment for the head and cover the top with card, like this—
3. Then cut out another compartment for the helmet, shaping it as shown in the diagram.
4. From the card cut out some shoulders, feet and two arms.
5. Then you can decorate him in any way you like with paints and odd bits and pieces—cotton wool, matchsticks, buttons, etc.

Space Spider

Equipment: *1 cheese box; paper; 1 cardboard egg box; pipe cleaners; pins.*

1. Cut two card discs, 2 cm ($\frac{1}{4}$ in) larger in diameter than the cheese box.
2. Cut to the centre of each disc, then fold each round to form two cones and stick them together.
3. Glue the top and bottom of the cheese box together, then glue the cones to each side.
4. Bend the pipe cleaners to the shape of legs and glue them to the body.
5. Cut out one of the egg box compartments and cut a slot into it so that it fits into the box, like this—
6. Add eyes and fangs from bits of pipe cleaner and card. Then paint the space spider.

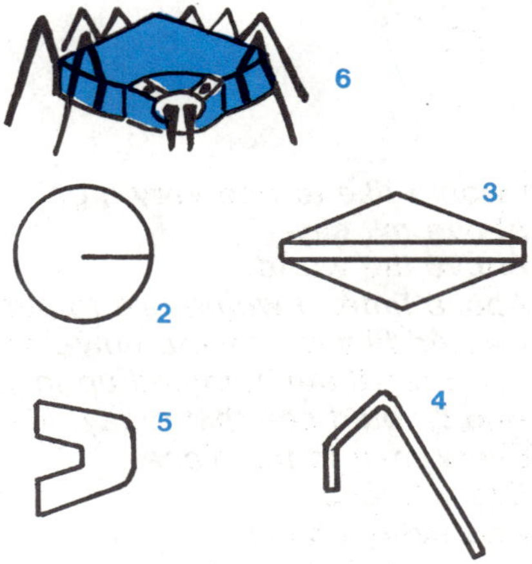

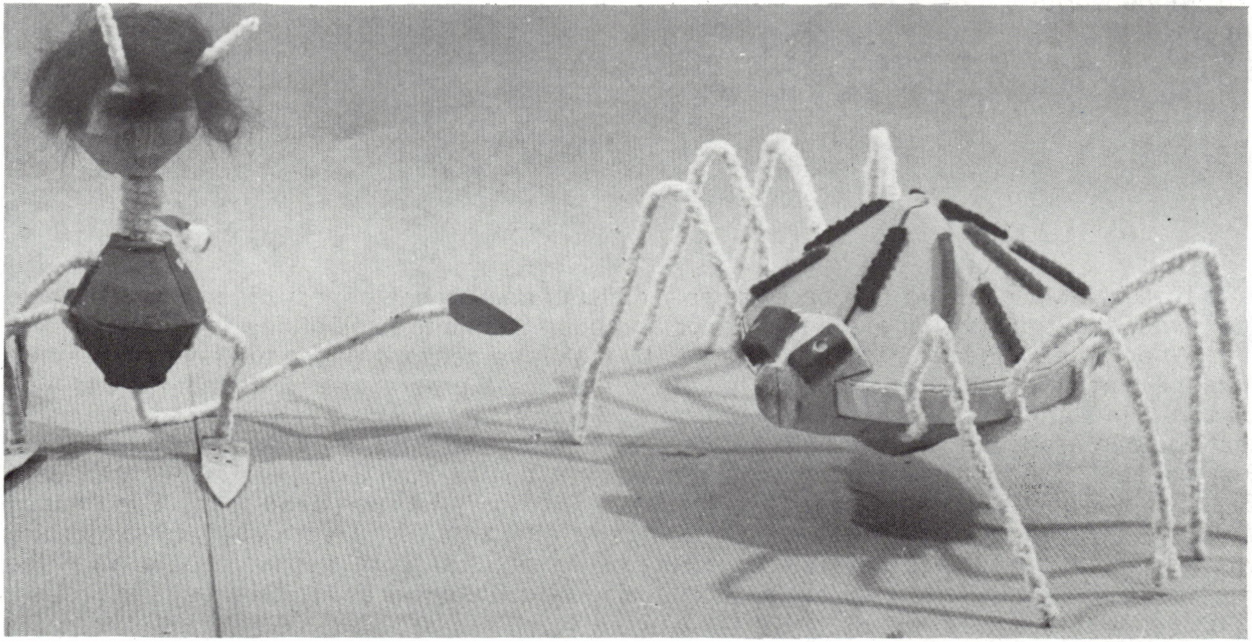

Programme Planning

I would like to rise very high, Lord,
Above my city
Above the world
Above time. I would like to purify my glance and borrow your eyes.
I would like to see the universe, humanity, history, as the Father sees them . . .
. . . Everything summed up in you, things on earth and things in heaven.
And I would see that today, like yesterday, the most minute details are the part of it.
Every man in his place
Every Group
And every object . . .
. . . Then, falling on my knees, I would admire, Lord, the mystery of this world . . .
. . . I would like to rise very high, Lord,
Above my city
Above the world
Above time
I would like to purify my glance and borrow your eyes.

Extracts from *Prayers of Life*
Michel Quoist

PROGRAMME planning can be extremely difficult, and probably most of us have, at some time, stared blankly at a sheet of paper and been unable to think of new ideas.

When an engineer plans a job, he starts by making a network, listing all the activities that must be carried out, and from this he is able to produce a programme. This method can also be useful in planning any activity for youngsters. Think of any object, and then find all the items that you can associate with the object. From the items found, further ideas will begin to form. For example, if the word is **'coffee',** coffee is a drink, comes from Brazil and needs transport. Brazil is a modern city surrounded by jungle. Apart from drink we need food. Food needs transport. Transport involves travelling by sea, air, rail or road. If we are going by sea or air, we need to know weather conditions. If we are using road transport, then we need to know the Highway Code. Using all forms of transport accidents could occur and a knowledge of first aid is essential.

As you can see from the list we have drawn up, a programme could easily be arranged around the word **'coffee'.**
Here are some possibilities:
Flag of Brazil—jungle scene or game—modern city—model aeroplane or game—model ship or game—railways—planning a journey—24 hour clock—Highway Code—first aid—food and drink.
From these ideas pick out suitable items for a balanced programme. The material in this book can be used to make up programmes for an evening, an afternoon or a Pack Holiday weekend. In each case, when planning a programme, always plan more activities than necessary; if an item is not going well an additional one can be used in its place.
In all programmes it is essential not only to set the scene at the start, but to explain the connection between the individual games or activities, and the main theme, thus continuing a story throughout.
Youngsters, when allowed, will use their imaginations to the full when acting a part. For example the boy who is acting the part of a pirate, will soon associate the football in a throwing game with a cannonball fired at his ship. Whilst the spaceman will see the ball as a meteor rushing towards his spacecraft. In simple relay, the Cub is flying an aircraft round the world, or a famous racing driver, out to win the Monte Carlo Rally.
What boy would not enjoy first aid if he were a flying doctor rushing to an emergency; or discovering nature if he was on an expedition into dark jungles, collecting specimens for a zoological society, or studying the stars in preparation for a journey to Mars . . . the examples are endless.
However it is up to the leader to create the right atmosphere and provide the stimulation that the youngsters require.
The programmes in this book deliberately contain more material than required and these could be spread over Pack meetings for several weeks. The stories at the beginning of each chapter should be elaborated and many more stories can be found along the same themes.
For those who find story telling difficult, here are a few hints:

1. First of all, only pick stories that you personally enjoy, children are very quick to spot if we are genuine. A simple story will do for a start and even a fairy story, providing it has a good moral, will go down well.
2. Memorise the basic facts, and it is important that these are stuck to rigidly, as youngsters will remember some of these, and even use them later in speaking amongst themselves.
The actual presentation need not be word for word, providing the main points come across, the dressing-up can be your own. A good example is **David Kossoff's** bible stories.
3. Drawings are also extremely useful, not only for putting the story across, but helping to remind you of the sequence. If you can draw them that is fine, if not, then show a picture from the book or pictures from newspapers, etc.
4. Sources of material:...*Daily Newspapers,*
Aesop's Fables,
The Bible,
Look and Learn—a children's weekly magazine,
Stories for Cub Scouts—Hazel Addis, available from the Scout Shop.

I hope that you will find the programmes useful, and that not only the Cubs, but you yourselves will have fun.

Acknowledgments

Prayers reproduced from *'Prayers of Life'* by **Michel Quoist** by permission of the publishers, **Gill and Macmillan, Dublin.**

The United States Embassy for the material on *Apollo 13.*

Many Scouters who have passed on ideas.